20 best
bridal shower recipes

Houghton Mifflin Harcourt
Boston • New York • 2013

Copyright © 2013 by General Mills, Minneapolis, Minnesota. All rights reserved.

Yoplait is a registered trademark of YOPLAIT MARQUES (France) used under license.

For information about permission to reproduce selections from this book, write to Permissions, Houghton Mifflin Harcourt Publishing Company, 215 Park Avenue South, New York, New York 10003.

www.hmhco.com

Cover photo: Bridal Shower Cakes (page 25)

General Mills
Food Content and Relationship Marketing Director: Geoff Johnson
Food Content Marketing Manager: Susan Klobuchar
Senior Editor: Grace Wells
Kitchen Manager: Ann Stuart
Recipe Development and Testing: Betty Crocker Kitchens
Photography: General Mills Photography Studios and Image Library

Houghton Mifflin Harcourt
Publisher: Natalie Chapman
Editorial Director: Cindy Kitchel
Executive Editor: Anne Ficklen
Associate Editor: Heather Dabah
Managing Editor: Rebecca Springer
Production Editor: Kristi Hart
Cover Design: Chrissy Kurpeski
Book Design: Tai Blanche

ISBN 978-0-544-31469-6
Printed in the United States of America

The Betty Crocker Kitchens seal guarantees success in your kitchen. Every recipe has been tested in America's Most Trusted Kitchens™ to meet our high standards of reliability, easy preparation and great taste.

FIND MORE GREAT IDEAS AT
Betty Crocker.com

Dear Friends,

This new collection of colorful mini books has been put together with you in mind because we know that you love great recipes and enjoy cooking and baking but have a busy lifestyle. So every little book in the series contains just 20 recipes for you to treasure and enjoy. Plus, each book is a single subject designed in a bite-size format just for you—it's easy to use and is filled with favorite recipes from the Betty Crocker Kitchens!

All of the books are conveniently divided into short chapters so you can quickly find what you're looking for, and the beautiful photos throughout are sure to entice you into making the delicious recipes. In the series, you'll discover a fabulous array of recipes to spark your interest—from cookies, cupcakes and birthday cakes to party ideas for a variety of occasions. There's grilled foods, potluck favorites and even gluten-free recipes too.

You'll love the variety in these mini books—so pick one or choose them all for your cooking pleasure.

Enjoy and happy cooking!

Sincerely,

Betty Crocker

contents

Savory Bites
Zucchini Appetizers • 6
Creamy Artichoke Appetizers • 7
Pea Pod Roll-Ups • 8
Crab Mini Quiches • 9
Filled Tomato Appetizers • 10
Cheesy Chicken 'n Spinach Pinwheels • 11

Sweet Bites
Bridal Shower Chex® Mix • 12
Mango-Lime Mini Cupcake Bites • 13
Cherry Mini Cupcakes • 14
Mini Royal Fruit Cakes • 15
Butterfly Cupcake Petits Fours • 16
Chocolate-Almond Cheesecake Bites • 17
Espresso Petits Fours • 18

Festive Desserts
Key Lime Yogurt Pie • 20
Praline-Crumb Caramel
    Cheesecake Bars • 21
Strawberry Shortcake Squares • 22
Engagement Ring Mini Cupcakes • 23
Double-Almond Cupcakes • 24
Bridal Shower Cakes • 25
Orange Cream Angel Food Cake • 26

Metric Conversion Guide • 36
Recipe Testing and Calculating Nutrition
    Information • 37

Savory Bites

Zucchini Appetizers

Prep Time: 15 Minutes • **Start to Finish:** 40 Minutes • Makes 48 appetizers

3 cups thinly sliced unpeeled zucchini (about 4 small)

1 cup Original Bisquick® mix

1 medium onion, finely chopped (½ cup)

½ cup grated Parmesan cheese

2 tablespoons chopped fresh parsley

½ teaspoon salt

½ teaspoon seasoned salt

½ teaspoon dried marjoram or oregano leaves

⅛ teaspoon pepper

1 clove garlic, finely chopped

½ cup vegetable oil

4 eggs, slightly beaten

Chopped fresh parsley, if desired

1 Heat oven to 350°F. Grease bottom and sides of 13 x 9-inch pan. In large bowl, stir all ingredients except parsley until well mixed. Spread in pan.

2 Bake 25 minutes or until golden brown. Cut into 6 rows by 4 rows, then cut squares diagonally in half into triangles. Sprinkle with chopped fresh parsley. Serve warm.

1 Appetizer: Calories 40; Total Fat 3g (Saturated Fat 1g, Trans Fat 0g); Cholesterol 20mg; Sodium 100mg; Total Carbohydrate 2g (Dietary Fiber 0g); Protein 1g

Tip "Slightly beaten" eggs are stirred until the yolks are broken and begin to blend with the whites. Beating the eggs before adding them to the other ingredients makes mixing the entire dish easier.

Creamy Artichoke Appetizers

Prep Time: 35 Minutes • **Start to Finish:** 1 Hour 10 Minutes • Makes 48 appetizers

3 cups Original Bisquick mix

1½ cups shredded mozzarella cheese (6 oz)

⅔ cup water

2 tablespoons vegetable oil

1½ cups mayonnaise

1½ cups grated Parmesan cheese

1 jar (7 oz) roasted red bell peppers, drained, diced

1 tablespoon Dijon mustard

1 tablespoon Worcestershire sauce

2 teaspoons garlic powder

2 cans (14 oz each) artichoke hearts, drained, chopped

1 Heat oven to 375°F. Spray 15 x 10 x 1-inch pan with cooking spray.

2 In large bowl, stir Bisquick mix and mozzarella cheese until thoroughly combined. Stir in water and oil until dough forms; beat vigorously 20 strokes. Let stand 8 minutes.

3 Using hands dipped in additional Bisquick mix, press dough in bottom and up sides of pan. Bake 9 to 11 minutes or until crust is puffed and top edges are just starting to brown.

4 Meanwhile, in medium bowl, mix all remaining ingredients except artichokes. Stir in artichokes. Spread mixture evenly over partially baked crust.

5 Bake 12 to 15 minutes or until thoroughly heated and crust is golden brown.

6 Set oven control to broil. Broil with top of pan 6 inches from heat 2 to 3 minutes or until filling is golden brown. Cool 10 minutes. Cut into 8 rows by 6 rows.

1 Appetizer: Calories 120; Total Fat 9g (Saturated Fat 2g, Trans Fat 0g); Cholesterol 5mg; Sodium 240mg; Total Carbohydrate 7g (Dietary Fiber 1g); Protein 3g **Carbohydrate Choices:** ½

Tip This recipe is all inclusive—no dippers needed. The dip is baked right into the crust!

Savory Bites

Pea Pod Roll-Ups

Prep Time: 20 Minutes • **Start to Finish:** 20 Minutes • Makes 24 roll-ups

6 oz fresh snow pea pods (24 to 30 pea pods)

⅓ cup salmon cream cheese spread (from 8-oz container)

1 to 2 teaspoons chopped fresh dill weed

24 pieces (½ x ¼ inch) red bell pepper, cucumber, carrot or red onion

1 In 1½- to 2-quart saucepan, heat 3 cups water to boiling; add pea pods. Cook uncovered 1 to 2 minutes or until bright green; drain. Immediately rinse with cold water; drain. Dry with paper towels.

2 Spread cream cheese over each pea pod; sprinkle with dill weed. Place 1 piece of bell pepper on center of each pea pod; bring ends of pea pod over filling, overlapping in center. Secure with toothpick.

1 Roll-Up: Calories 15; Total Fat 1g (Saturated Fat 0.5g, Trans Fat 0g); Cholesterol 0mg; Sodium 25mg; Total Carbohydrate 0g (Dietary Fiber 0g); Protein 0g **Carbohydrate Choices:** 0

Tip If you use carrots, cook them with the pea pods to brighten the color and soften them slightly.

Crab Mini Quiches

Prep Time: 15 Minutes • **Start to Finish:** 40 Minutes • Makes 24 mini quiches

- 1¼ cups Original Bisquick mix
- ¼ cup butter or margarine, softened
- 2 tablespoons boiling water
- ⅓ cup canned crabmeat, finely chopped cooked crabmeat or finely chopped imitation crabmeat
- ½ cup half-and-half
- 1 egg
- 2 medium green onions, thinly sliced (2 tablespoons)
- ¼ teaspoon salt
- ¼ teaspoon ground red pepper (cayenne)
- ½ cup shredded Parmesan cheese

1 Heat oven to 375°F. Spray 24 mini muffin cups with cooking spray. In small bowl, stir Bisquick mix and butter until blended. Add boiling water; stir vigorously until soft dough forms. Press rounded teaspoonful of dough on bottom and up side of each muffin cup. Divide crabmeat evenly among muffin cups.

2 In small bowl, beat half-and-half and egg with spoon until blended. Stir in onions, salt and red pepper. Spoon 1½ teaspoons egg mixture into each muffin cup. Sprinkle cheese over tops.

3 Bake about 20 minutes or until edges are golden brown and centers are set. Cool 5 minutes. Loosen sides of quiches from pan; remove from pan.

1 Mini Quiche: Calories 60; Total Fat 4g (Saturated Fat 2.5g, Trans Fat 0g); Cholesterol 20mg; Sodium 160mg; Total Carbohydrate 5g (Dietary Fiber 0g); Protein 2g **Carbohydrate Choices:** ½

Tip To make these mini quiches one day ahead, after baking, remove them from the muffin pan and place them on a cooling rack to cool. Cover; refrigerate. To serve, place the quiches on a cookie sheet; cover loosely with foil. Bake at 375°F 9 to 11 minutes or until hot.

Filled Tomato Appetizers

Prep Time: 35 Minutes • **Start to Finish:** 35 Minutes • Makes 24 appetizers

24 cherry tomatoes

Green onion tops, cut into 1¼-inch strips

½ cup chicken salad (from deli)

2 tablespoons prepared horseradish

1 With sharp knife, cut ¼ inch off stem side of each tomato and ⅛ inch off bottom. Using melon baller or small spoon, remove insides of tomatoes; discard.

2 Make cuts in ends of each green onion piece; place in bowl of ice water until curly.

3 In small bowl, mix chicken salad and horseradish. Spoon 1 teaspoon chicken salad into each tomato. Place 1 green onion brush in top center of each tomato for stem.

1 Appetizer: Calories 15; Total Fat 0.5g (Saturated Fat 0g, Trans Fat 0g); Cholesterol 0mg; Sodium 15mg; Total Carbohydrate 1g (Dietary Fiber 0g); Protein 0g **Carbohydrate Choices:** 0

Tip A narrow baby spoon works well to spoon the chicken salad into each tomato.

Cheesy Chicken 'n Spinach Pinwheels

Prep Time: 25 Minutes • **Start to Finish:** 40 Minutes • Makes 20 pinwheels

- 1 box (9 oz) frozen chopped spinach
- 1 tablespoon olive oil
- ¼ cup finely chopped onion (1 small)
- 1 clove garlic, finely chopped
- 2 slices bacon, crisply cooked, crumbled
- ½ cup finely chopped cooked chicken
- ¾ cup shredded Asiago cheese
- ¼ cup mayonnaise or salad dressing
- 1 can (8 oz) refrigerated crescent seamless dough sheet
- 1 egg, beaten

1 Heat oven to 375°F. Spray cookie sheet with cooking spray. Cook spinach in microwave as directed on box. Drain spinach in strainer; cool 5 minutes. Carefully squeeze with paper towel to drain well.

2 In 10-inch skillet, heat oil over medium heat. Add onion and garlic; cook 2 to 3 minutes, stirring occasionally, until crisp-tender. Remove from heat. Stir in spinach, bacon, chicken, cheese and mayonnaise.

3 Unroll dough on work surface. Spread spinach mixture on rectangle to within ½ inch of edges. Starting at long side of rectangle, roll up; seal long edge. With serrated knife, cut into 20 slices. Place slices cut side down on cookie sheet. Brush with egg.

4 Bake 10 to 15 minutes or until golden brown. Remove from cookie sheet. Serve warm.

1 Pinwheel: Calories 100; Total Fat 7g (Saturated Fat 2.5g, Trans Fat 0g); Cholesterol 20mg; Sodium 180mg; Total Carbohydrate 6g (Dietary Fiber 0g); Protein 3g **Carbohydrate Choices:** ½

Bridal Shower Chex Mix

Prep Time: 15 Minutes • **Start to Finish:** 15 Minutes • Makes 26 servings (½ cup each)

6 cups Honey Nut Chex® cereal

12 oz vanilla-flavored candy coating (almond bark)

2 tablespoons vegetable oil

2 packages (5 oz each) white fudge–covered pretzels

1½ cups white candy-coated almonds

1 Line 15 x 10 x 1-inch pan with waxed paper or foil. In large bowl, place cereal.

2 In medium microwavable bowl, place candy coating and oil. Microwave uncovered on High 1 minute; stir. Microwave on High 20 seconds longer if necessary until coating is melted. Pour over cereal, stirring until evenly coated. Spread in pan. Refrigerate 4 to 6 minutes or until candy coating is set.

3 Break into bite-size pieces in large bowl. Stir in pretzels and almonds.

1 Serving: Calories 220; Total Fat 9g (Saturated Fat 3.5g, Trans Fat 0g); Cholesterol 0mg; Sodium 180mg; Total Carbohydrate 32g (Dietary Fiber 1g); Protein 3g **Carbohydrate Choices:** 2

Tip Use candy-coated almonds in colors to match the bridal party colors. Then, pack in small decorative boxes for each guest to take home.

Mango-Lime Mini Cupcake Bites

Prep Time: 30 Minutes • **Start to Finish:** 1 Hour 10 Minutes • Makes 24 mini cupcake bites

Cupcakes

1 cup Gold Medal® all-purpose flour
1 teaspoon baking powder
⅛ teaspoon salt
¼ cup unsalted butter, softened
⅓ cup granulated sugar
2 eggs
⅓ cup milk
1 teaspoon grated lime peel
½ cup finely chopped mango (½ medium)

Frosting

¼ cup unsalted butter, softened
2 cups powdered sugar
½ teaspoon grated lime peel
2 tablespoons fresh lime juice

1 Heat oven to 350°F. Place mini paper baking cup in each of 24 mini muffin cups; spray paper cups with cooking spray. In small bowl, mix flour, baking powder and salt; set aside.

2 In medium bowl, beat ¼ cup butter and the granulated sugar with electric mixer on medium speed 1 minute. Add eggs, one at a time, beating on low speed after each addition. Alternately add flour mixture, about one-third at a time, and ⅓ cup milk, about half at a time, beating just until blended. Beat in 1 teaspoon lime peel. Stir in mango.

3 Divide batter evenly among muffin cups, filling each with about 1 tablespoon plus 1 teaspoon batter.

4 Bake 12 minutes or until toothpick inserted in center comes out clean. Cool 10 minutes. Remove cupcakes from pans; place on cooling racks. Cool completely, about 15 minutes.

5 In medium bowl, beat all frosting ingredients with electric mixer on medium speed until smooth. Spoon frosting into decorating bag fitted with star tip; pipe frosting on each cupcake.

1 Mini Cupcake Bite: Calories 120; Total Fat 4.5g (Saturated Fat 2.5g, Trans Fat 0g); Cholesterol 30mg; Sodium 40mg; Total Carbohydrate 18g (Dietary Fiber 0g); Protein 1g **Carbohydrate Choices:** 1

Tip You can replace the lime with lemon in this recipe, but do not remove citrus entirely as it balances the sweetness of the mango.

Cherry Mini Cupcakes

Prep Time: 1 Hour 50 Minutes • **Start to Finish:** 1 Hour 50 Minutes • Makes 58 mini cupcakes

Cupcakes

1 box Betty Crocker® Super-Moist® white cake mix

Water, vegetable oil and egg whites called for on cake mix box

1 package (0.13 oz) cherry-flavored unsweetened soft drink mix

1 teaspoon almond extract

Glaze

1 bag (2 lb) powdered sugar (8 cups)

½ cup water

½ cup corn syrup

2 teaspoons almond extract

2 to 3 teaspoons hot water

Decoration

Miniature red candy hearts

1 Heat oven to 375°F (350°F for dark or nonstick pans). Grease bottoms only of 58 mini muffin cups. In large bowl, beat all cupcake ingredients with electric mixer on low speed 30 seconds, then on medium speed 2 minutes, scraping bowl occasionally.

2 Divide batter evenly among muffin cups, filling each about half full. (Cover and refrigerate remaining batter until ready to bake; cool pan before reusing.)

3 Bake 10 to 13 minutes or until toothpick inserted in center comes out clean. Cool 5 minutes. Remove cupcakes from pans; place on cooling racks. Cool completely, about 30 minutes.

4 Place cooling rack on cookie sheet or waxed paper to catch glaze drips. In 3-quart saucepan, mix all glaze ingredients except hot water. Heat over low heat, stirring frequently, until sugar is dissolved. Remove from heat. Stir in 2 teaspoons hot water. If necessary, stir in up to 1 teaspoon more water so glaze will just coat cupcakes.

5 Turn each cupcake top side down on cooling rack. Pour about 1 tablespoon glaze over each cupcake, letting glaze coat sides. Let stand until glaze is set, about 15 minutes.

6 Top each cupcake with candy hearts. Store loosely covered.

1 Mini Cupcake (Cake and Glaze Only): Calories 110; Total Fat 1.5g (Saturated Fat 0g, Trans Fat 0g); Cholesterol 0mg; Sodium 60mg; Total Carbohydrate 24g (Dietary Fiber 0g); Protein 0g **Carbohydrate Choices:** 1½

Tip Bake the mini cupcakes up to 2 weeks ahead of time and freeze. Add the glaze when it's time for the party.

Mini Royal Fruit Cakes

Prep Time: 1 Hour 30 Minutes • **Start to Finish:** 18 Hours 30 Minutes • Makes 96 mini cakes

1 cup currants
1 cup golden raisins
½ cup dried cranberries
½ cup brandy
1 orange
1 lemon
1 cup butter, softened
¼ cup molasses
1 cup packed brown sugar
4 eggs, lightly beaten
1½ cups Gold Medal all-purpose flour
3 tablespoons brandy
4 containers (1 lb each) Betty Crocker Rich & Creamy creamy white or vanilla frosting
Edible fresh flowers, if desired
Fresh mint, if desired

1 In large bowl, place currants, golden raisins and dried cranberries. Zest and juice orange; add to bowl. Zest and juice lemon; add to bowl. Pour in ½ cup brandy, mix well. Cover with plastic wrap; let stand overnight. Drain extra liquid off soaked fruit, if needed.

2 Heat oven to 325°F. Grease and flour 13 x 9-inch pan. In large bowl, beat butter, molasses and sugar with electric mixer on medium speed, scraping bowl occasionally until blended. Gradually add eggs and flour, alternating until both are incorporated. Stir in soaked fruit. Spread into pan.

3 Bake 50 to 55 minutes or until toothpick inserted in center comes out clean and surface is deep golden brown. Cool in pan 2 hours. Brush with remaining 3 tablespoons brandy. Remove from pan.

4 Cut cake into 12 rows by 8 rows. Place cooling rack on cookie sheet or waxed paper to catch glaze drips. Place 24 squares, leaving space between each, on cooling rack.

5 In medium microwavable bowl, place frosting from 1 container. Microwave on High in 30-second increments, stirring until smooth and pourable. Quickly spoon about 1 tablespoon frosting over each of 24 mini cakes, covering tops and letting frosting drip over sides. Reheat frosting, if necessary. Repeat with remaining frosting and mini cakes. Let stand about 30 minutes or until frosting is set. Decorate with edible fresh flowers and mint. Store loosely covered.

1 Mini Cake: Calories 130; Total Fat 5g (Saturated Fat 2g, Trans Fat 1g); Cholesterol 15mg; Sodium 60mg; Total Carbohydrate 20g (Dietary Fiber 0g); Protein 0g **Carbohydrate Choices:** 1

Tip For extra brandy flavor, wrap the undecorated cake in foil and let stand for up to 2 weeks. Unwrap and sprinkle with 1 tablespoon additional brandy each week.

Butterfly Cupcake Petits Fours

Prep Time: 2 Hours 30 Minutes • **Start to Finish:** 3 Hours 20 Minutes • Makes 72 cupcake petits fours

Cupcakes

2¾ cups Gold Medal all-purpose flour
3 teaspoons baking powder
½ teaspoon salt
¾ cup shortening
1⅔ cups granulated sugar
5 egg whites
2½ teaspoons vanilla
1¼ cups milk

Glaze

8 cups powdered sugar
½ cup water
½ cup light corn syrup
2 teaspoons almond extract

Decorations

Pastel-colored candy-coated chocolate candies
Small yogurt-covered pretzel twists
Black string licorice, cut into ½-inch pieces

1 Heat oven to 350°F. Place mini paper baking cup in each of 24 mini muffin cups.

2 In medium bowl, mix flour, baking powder and salt; set aside. In large bowl, beat shortening with electric mixer on medium speed 30 seconds. Gradually add granulated sugar, about ⅓ cup at a time, beating well after each addition. Beat 2 minutes longer. Add egg whites, one at a time, beating well after each addition. Beat in vanilla. On low speed, alternately add flour mixture, about one-third at a time, and milk, about half at a time, beating just until blended.

3 Divide batter evenly among muffin cups, filling each about two-thirds full. (Cover and refrigerate remaining batter until ready to bake; cool pan before reusing.)

4 Bake 12 to 16 minutes or until golden brown and toothpick inserted in center comes out clean. Cool 5 minutes. Remove cupcakes from pans; place on cooling racks. Cool completely, about 15 minutes. Repeat with remaining batter if necessary to make additional cupcakes.

5 In 2½ quart saucepan, beat all glaze ingredients until smooth. Heat over low heat just until lukewarm. Remove from heat. If necessary, add hot water, a few drops at a time, until glaze is pourable.

6 Remove paper baking cups from cupcakes; turn cupcakes upside down on cooling rack over large bowl. Working with 1 cupcake at a time, pour enough glaze over top to cover top and sides. Reheat glaze, if necessary. Place 4 pastel candies in a row in center of each cupcake. Place 2 pretzels, 1 on each side of the row of candies, to look like wings. Add 2 licorice pieces for antennae.

1 Cupcake Petit Four: Calories 120; Total Fat 2.5g (Saturated Fat 0.5g, Trans Fat 0g); Cholesterol 0mg; Sodium 45mg; Total Carbohydrate 24g (Dietary Fiber 0g); Protein 1g **Carbohydrate Choices:** 1½

Tip For sparkly butterfly wings, brush pretzels with a little of the glaze, then sprinkle with colored sugar.

Chocolate-Almond Cheesecake Bites

Prep Time: 50 Minutes • **Start to Finish:** 3 Hours 30 Minutes • Makes 48 cheesecake bites

Crust

16 thin chocolate wafer cookies (from 9-oz package), crushed (1 cup)

¼ cup butter, melted

Filling

1 package (8 oz) cream cheese, softened

¼ cup sour cream

¼ cup sugar

1 egg

¼ teaspoon almond extract

Coating

2⅓ cups semisweet chocolate chips

3 tablespoons shortening

2 oz vanilla-flavored candy coating (almond bark), chopped

1 teaspoon vegetable oil

1 Heat oven to 300°F. Cut 14 x 12-inch sheet of heavy-duty foil; line 8-inch square pan with foil so foil extends over sides of pan. Spray foil with cooking spray. In small bowl, mix all crust ingredients. Press in bottom of pan.

2 In large bowl, beat cream cheese, sour cream and sugar with electric mixer on medium speed until fluffy. Beat in egg and almond extract, scraping bowl if necessary. Pour over crust.

3 Bake 30 to 40 minutes or until edges are set (center will be soft but will set when cool). Cool 1 hour. Cover; refrigerate 1 hour. Meanwhile, cover 2 cookie sheets with waxed paper.

4 Using foil, lift cheesecake out of pan. Cut into 8 rows by 6 rows. In 1-quart microwavable bowl, microwave chocolate chips and shortening uncovered on Medium (50%) 3 minutes. Stir; microwave in 15-second increments, stirring after each, until melted and smooth.

5 Work with half of bites at a time (24 bites); refrigerate other half until needed. Place 1 bite on fork and dip fork into chocolate to coat. Lift fork from chocolate and allow excess chocolate to drain off. Place on cookie sheet. Repeat with remaining cheesecake bites.

6 In small microwavable bowl, microwave candy coating and oil uncovered on High 1 minute. Stir; microwave in 15-second increments, stirring after each, until melted. Spoon into small resealable food-storage plastic bag. Seal bag; cut tiny hole in corner of bag. Squeeze bag to pipe melted coating over dipped bites. Store covered in refrigerator.

1 Cheesecake Bite: Calories 100; Total Fat 7g (Saturated Fat 4g, Trans Fat 0g); Cholesterol 15mg; Sodium 40mg; Total Carbohydrate 9g (Dietary Fiber 0g); Protein 1g **Carbohydrate Choices:** ½

Tip If the chocolate coating cools and starts to get thick, microwave on High for 10 to 15 seconds to soften it.

Espresso Petits Fours

Prep Time: 1 Hour • **Start to Finish:** 2 Hours 50 Minutes • Makes 35 petits fours

Cake

3 eggs, separated
¾ cup granulated sugar
½ cup butter, melted
1⅓ cups Gold Medal all-purpose flour
1 teaspoon baking powder
¼ teaspoon salt
⅓ cup water
1 teaspoon instant espresso coffee powder or granules

Filling

3 tablespoons coffee-flavored liqueur
½ cup butter, softened
1½ cups powdered sugar
½ teaspoon vanilla
½ cup toasted sliced almonds

Icing

2 cups powdered sugar
3 tablespoons coffee-flavored liqueur
2 tablespoons cornstarch
1 tablespoon butter, melted
1 to 2 teaspoons water

Garnish

35 small espresso coffee beans
35 toasted sliced almonds

1 Heat oven to 350°F. Grease 13 x 9-inch pan with shortening; lightly flour. In medium bowl, beat egg whites with electric mixer on high speed until stiff peaks form, gradually adding ¼ cup of the granulated sugar. Set aside.

2 In large bowl, beat 3 egg yolks, remaining ½ cup granulated sugar and ½ cup melted butter at medium speed until creamy. Add flour, baking powder and salt. Mix on low speed until moistened. (Batter will be thick.) In small bowl, mix ⅓ cup water and espresso powder; add to batter. Beat at low speed until blended. Beat at medium speed until smooth. Fold in beaten egg whites. Spread in pan.

3 Bake 18 to 23 minutes or until top springs back when touched lightly in center. Cool 10 minutes. Run knife around edges to loosen; turn cake upside down onto cooling rack. Place another cooling rack on cake and turn upside down so top of cake is upright. Cool completely, about 30 minutes. Cover loosely; freeze 15 minutes or refrigerate 30 minutes.

4 With long thin serrated knife, cut cake horizontally in half. Brush 3 tablespoons liqueur over cut side of bottom half. In small bowl, beat ½ cup butter, 1½ cups powdered sugar and the vanilla with electric mixer on low speed until mixed. Beat at medium speed until smooth and creamy. Place ½ cup almonds in food processor with metal blade. Process 10 to 15 seconds or until finely chopped. Stir into filling. Spread filling evenly over bottom half of cake. Place top of cake over filling, cut side down. Press down firmly. Cover with plastic wrap; freeze 15 minutes.

5 Meanwhile, in medium bowl, beat all icing ingredients except water on low speed until smooth, adding water if necessary for drizzling consistency. Remove cake from freezer. Trim outside edges of cake to create 10½ x 7½-inch rectangle. Cut into 7 rows by 5 rows. Place squares on 2 large cooling racks set over sheets of waxed paper. Using fork or spoon, drizzle and slightly spread each cake with icing. Top each with 1 coffee bean and 1 sliced almond. Let set, about 15 minutes. Flatten 35 mini paper baking cups slightly. Place 1 petit four on each paper. Cover loosely to store.

1 Petit Four: Calories 160; Total Fat 7g (Saturated Fat 3.5g, Trans Fat 0g); Cholesterol 30mg; Sodium 85mg; Total Carbohydrate 22g (Dietary Fiber 0g); Protein 1g **Carbohydrate Choices:** 1½

Tip To toast almonds, spread in ungreased shallow pan. Bake uncovered at 350°F 6 to 10 minutes, stirring occasionally, until light brown. For the almonds in the filling and the garnish, toast a total of about 1 cup. Pick out the prettiest 35 slices for the top garnish, and use ½ cup for the filling. Keep any remaining almonds for topping salads or other desserts.

Festive Desserts

Key Lime Yogurt Pie

Prep Time: 15 Minutes • **Start to Finish:** 2 Hours 15 Minutes • Makes 8 servings

- 2 tablespoons cold water
- 1 tablespoon fresh lime juice
- 1½ teaspoons unflavored gelatin
- 4 oz (half of 8-oz package) fat-free cream cheese, softened
- 3 containers (6 oz each) Yoplait® Light Thick & Creamy Key lime pie yogurt
- ½ cup frozen (thawed) reduced-fat whipped topping
- 2 teaspoons grated lime peel
- 1 reduced-fat graham cracker crumb crust (6 oz)

1 In 1-quart saucepan, mix water and lime juice. Sprinkle gelatin on lime juice mixture; let stand 1 minute. Heat over low heat, stirring constantly, until gelatin is dissolved. Cool slightly, about 2 minutes.

2 In medium bowl, beat cream cheese with electric mixer on medium speed until smooth. Add yogurt and lime juice mixture; beat on low speed until well blended.

3 Fold in whipped topping and lime peel. Pour into crust. Refrigerate until set, about 2 hours.

1 Serving: Calories 160; Total Fat 4g (Saturated Fat 1.5g, Trans Fat 1g); Cholesterol 0mg; Sodium 210mg; Total Carbohydrate 26g (Dietary Fiber 0g); Protein 5g **Carbohydrate Choices:** 2

Praline-Crumb Caramel Cheesecake Bars

Prep Time: 25 Minutes • **Start to Finish:** 3 Hours 35 Minutes • Makes 36 bars

- 1 pouch (1 lb 1.5 oz) Betty Crocker sugar cookie mix
- ½ cup cold butter or margarine
- 2 packages (8 oz each) cream cheese, softened
- ½ cup sugar
- 2 tablespoons Gold Medal all-purpose flour
- ½ cup caramel topping
- 1 teaspoon vanilla
- 1 egg
- ½ cup chopped pecans
- ½ cup toffee bits

1 Heat oven to 350°F. Grease bottom and sides of 13 x 9-inch pan. In large bowl, place cookie mix. Cut in butter, using pastry blender or fork, until mixture is crumbly. Reserve 1½ cups mixture for topping. Press remaining mixture in bottom of pan. Bake 10 minutes.

2 In medium bowl, beat cream cheese, sugar, flour, ¼ cup of the caramel topping, the vanilla and egg until smooth.

3 Spread cream cheese mixture evenly over partially baked cookie base. Sprinkle with reserved 1½ cups crumb topping, the pecans and toffee bits.

4 Bake 35 to 40 minutes. Cool 30 minutes. Refrigerate about 2 hours or until chilled. Drizzle with remaining ¼ cup caramel topping. Store covered in refrigerator.

1 Bar: Calories 190; Total Fat 11g (Saturated Fat 5g, Trans Fat 1g); Cholesterol 30mg; Sodium 125mg; Total Carbohydrate 21g (Dietary Fiber 0g); Protein 1g
Carbohydrate Choices: 1½

Strawberry Shortcake Squares

Prep Time: 15 Minutes • **Start to Finish:** 1 Hour 50 Minutes • Makes 15 squares

Cake

3 cups Original Bisquick mix
1 cup granulated sugar
¼ cup butter or margarine, softened
1 cup milk
2 teaspoons vanilla
2 eggs

Topping

1 cup whipping cream
1 package (8 oz) cream cheese, softened
⅓ cup powdered sugar
1 teaspoon vanilla
6 cups sliced fresh strawberries (about 2 lb)
Fresh mint sprigs, if desired

1 Heat oven to 350°F. Grease bottom and sides of 13 x 9-inch pan with shortening and lightly flour, or spray with baking spray with flour. In large bowl, beat all cake ingredients with electric mixer on low speed 30 seconds. Beat on medium speed 2 minutes, scraping bowl occasionally. Pour into pan.

2 Bake 30 to 35 minutes or until toothpick inserted in center comes out clean. Cool completely, about 1 hour.

3 In chilled small bowl, beat whipping cream with electric mixer on high speed until soft peaks form; set aside. In medium bowl, beat cream cheese, powdered sugar and 1 teaspoon vanilla on medium speed until well blended. Fold in whipped cream. Spread topping over cake. Refrigerate up to 6 hours, if desired.

4 Cut into 5 rows by 3 rows. Place on individual dessert plates. Top with strawberries. Garnish with mint.

1 Serving: Calories 340; Total Fat 18g (Saturated Fat 10g, Trans Fat 0g); Cholesterol 0mg; Sodium 380mg; Total Carbohydrate 38g (Dietary Fiber 2g); Protein 5g **Carbohydrate Choices:** 2½

Engagement Ring Mini Cupcakes

Prep Time: 20 Minutes • **Start to Finish:** 1 Hour 10 Minutes • Makes 58 mini cupcakes

1 box Betty Crocker SuperMoist white cake mix

Water, vegetable oil and egg whites called for on cake mix box

2 cups powdered sugar

3 to 4 tablespoons milk

Assorted colored rock candy

1 Heat oven to 350°F (325°F for dark or nonstick pans). Place paper baking cup in each of 58 mini muffin cups.

2 Make cake batter as directed on box. Divide batter evenly among muffin cups, filling each about two-thirds full. (Cover and refrigerate remaining batter until ready to bake; cool pan before reusing.)

3 Bake 11 to 14 minutes or until toothpick inserted in center comes out clean. Cool 5 minutes. Remove cupcakes from pan; place on cooling rack. Cool completely, about 30 minutes.

4 In small bowl, stir powdered sugar and 3 tablespoons milk until smooth. Add additional milk, 1 teaspoon at a time, until desired spreading consistency. Frost cupcakes. Top with rock candy pieces. Store loosely covered.

1 Mini Cupcake: Calories 70; Total Fat 1.5g (Saturated Fat 0g, Trans Fat 0g); Cholesterol 0mg; Sodium 60mg; Total Carbohydrate 13g (Dietary Fiber 0g); Protein 0g **Carbohydrate Choices:** 1

Tip Using a scoop makes spooning cupcake batter quick, less messy and also ensures that cupcakes will be the same size. Use a #70 or small-sized spring-loaded ice cream scoop that is equal to about 1 tablespoon.

Double-Almond Cupcakes

Prep Time: 30 Minutes • **Start to Finish:** 1 Hour 30 Minutes • Makes 18 cupcakes

Cupcakes

1 box Betty Crocker Super-Moist white cake mix

Water, vegetable oil and egg whites called for on cake mix box

1 tablespoon almond extract

Frosting

1¼ cups butter, softened

2½ cups powdered sugar

2 tablespoons whipping cream

2 teaspoons almond extract

Garnish

Jordan almonds, if desired

1 Heat oven to 350°F (325°F for dark or nonstick pans). Place paper baking cup in each of 18 regular-size muffin cups. Make cake batter as directed on box, using water, oil and egg whites, and adding 1 tablespoon almond extract. Divide batter evenly among muffin cups, filling each about three-fourths full.

2 Bake 20 to 25 minutes or until toothpick inserted in center comes out clean. Cool 10 minutes. Remove cupcakes from pans; place on cooling racks. Cool completely, about 30 minutes.

3 In medium bowl, beat butter and powdered sugar with electric mixer on low speed until blended. Add whipping cream and 2 teaspoons almond extract; beat on high speed until well blended. Spoon frosting into decorating bag fitted with #46 tip. Using tip, with smooth side facing down, generously pipe frosting in circular motion. Store loosely covered.

1 Cupcake: Calories 330; Total Fat 18g (Saturated Fat 10g, Trans Fat 0.5g); Cholesterol 35mg; Sodium 280mg; Total Carbohydrate 37g (Dietary Fiber 0g); Protein 2g **Carbohydrate Choices:** 2½

Tip Tint frosting with water-based food color to match the bridal party's colors. Then, wrap each cupcake in a laser-cut cupcake wrap or other decorative wrap.

Bridal Shower Cakes

Prep Time: 40 Minutes • **Start to Finish:** 3 Hours 25 Minutes • Makes 16 servings

1 box Betty Crocker Super-Moist cake mix (any flavor)

Water, vegetable oil and eggs called for on cake mix box

1 can (8.4 oz) white cupcake icing

1 can (8.4 oz) pink cupcake icing

White decorating decors, as desired

1 can (6.4 oz) black decorating icing

1 can (6.4 oz) white decorating icing

1 can (6.4 oz) red decorating icing

1 Heat oven to 350°F. Grease bottoms only of 2 (8-inch) heart-shaped foil pans. Make cake batter as directed on box. Pour into pans. Bake as directed on box for 2 (8-inch) rounds.

2 Cool 10 minutes. Run knife around sides of pans to loosen cakes; remove from pans to cooling racks. Cool completely, about 1 hour.

3 For bride cake, place 1 cake layer on serving plate. Frost cake with white cupcake icing, leaving V-shaped area at top of cake. Frost V-shaped area with pink cupcake icing. Using white cupcake icing with writing tip, pipe lace design on dress and V-shaped edge of dress. Use white decorating decors to make pearl necklace.

4 For groom cake, place remaining cake layer on another serving plate. Frost cake with black decorating icing, leaving V-shaped area at top of cake. Frost V-shaped area with white decorating icing. Pipe black buttons and lapels with black decorating icing. Pipe red bow tie on shirt with red decorating icing. Store loosely covered at room temperature.

1 Serving: Calories 340; Total Fat 14g (Saturated Fat 2.5g, Trans Fat 1g); Cholesterol 0mg; Sodium 250mg; Total Carbohydrate 53g (Dietary Fiber 0g); Protein 2g **Carbohydrate Choices:** 3½

Tip For a bridal shower, decorate one cake for the bride. Instead of making the groom cake, decorate that cake similar to the bride cake but use icing colors of the bridesmaid's dresses.

Orange Cream Angel Food Cake

Prep Time: 35 Minutes • **Start to Finish:** 5 Hours 25 Minutes • Makes 12 servings

Cake

1 box Betty Crocker white angel food cake mix

1¼ cups cold water

Orange Cream

6 egg yolks

1 cup sugar

2 teaspoons cornstarch

⅔ cup orange juice

Dash salt

¾ cup butter or margarine, cut into pieces

1 cup whipping cream

1 tablespoon grated orange peel

Orange peel twists, if desired

1 Move oven rack to lowest position (remove other racks). Heat oven to 350°F. In extra-large glass or metal bowl, beat cake mix and cold water with electric mixer on low speed 30 seconds. Beat on medium speed 1 minute. Pour into ungreased 10-inch angel food (tube) cake pan. (Do not use fluted tube cake pan or 9-inch angel food pan or batter will overflow.)

2 Bake 37 to 47 minutes or until top is dark golden brown and cracks feel very dry and are not sticky. Do not underbake. Immediately turn pan upside down onto heatproof funnel or bottle until cake is completely cool, about 2 hours.

3 Meanwhile, in 2-quart saucepan, beat egg yolks, sugar, cornstarch, orange juice and salt with whisk until blended. Add butter; cook 2 to 3 minutes over medium heat, stirring frequently, until boiling. Boil 3 to 5 minutes, stirring constantly, until thickened and mixture coats the back of a spoon. Immediately pour orange cream mixture through fine-mesh strainer into medium bowl. Cover with plastic wrap, pressing wrap directly onto surface of orange cream. Refrigerate about 1 hour or until completely chilled.

4 In medium bowl, beat whipping cream on high speed until stiff peaks form. Fold whipped cream and grated orange peel into orange cream.

5 On serving plate, place cake with browned side down. Cut off top one-third of cake, using long, sharp knife; set aside. Scoop out 1-inch-wide and 1-inch-deep tunnel around cake. Set aside scooped-out cake for another use. Spoon 1⅓ cups orange cream into tunnel. Replace top of cake to seal filling. Frost top and side of cake with remaining orange cream. Refrigerate at least 2 hours before serving. Garnish with orange twists. Store covered in refrigerator.

1 Serving: Calories 420; Total Fat 21g (Saturated Fat 13g, Trans Fat 0.5g); Cholesterol 160mg; Sodium 410mg; Total Carbohydrate 51g (Dietary Fiber 0g); Protein 5g **Carbohydrate Choices:** 3½

Tip When frosting this cake, first seal in the crumbs by spreading a thin layer of orange cream around the side of the cake. Then frost the top and go back over the side for complete coverage.

Metric Conversion Guide

Volume

U.S. Units	Canadian Metric	Australian Metric
¼ teaspoon	1 mL	1 ml
½ teaspoon	2 mL	2 ml
1 teaspoon	5 mL	5 ml
1 tablespoon	15 mL	20 ml
¼ cup	50 mL	60 ml
⅓ cup	75 mL	80 ml
½ cup	125 mL	125 ml
⅔ cup	150 mL	170 ml
¾ cup	175 mL	190 ml
1 cup	250 mL	250 ml
1 quart	1 liter	1 liter
1½ quarts	1.5 liters	1.5 liters
2 quarts	2 liters	2 liters
2½ quarts	2.5 liters	2.5 liters
3 quarts	3 liters	3 liters
4 quarts	4 liters	4 liters

Weight

U.S. Units	Canadian Metric	Australian Metric
1 ounce	30 grams	30 grams
2 ounces	55 grams	60 grams
3 ounces	85 grams	90 grams
4 ounces (¼ pound)	115 grams	125 grams
8 ounces (½ pound)	225 grams	225 grams
16 ounces (1 pound)	455 grams	500 grams
1 pound	455 grams	0.5 kilogram

Note: The recipes in this cookbook have not been developed or tested using metric measures. When converting recipes to metric, some variations in quality may be noted.

Measurements

Inches	Centimeters
1	2.5
2	5.0
3	7.5
4	10.0
5	12.5
6	15.0
7	17.5
8	20.5
9	23.0
10	25.5
11	28.0
12	30.5
13	33.0

Temperatures

Fahrenheit	Celsius
32°	0°
212°	100°
250°	120°
275°	140°
300°	150°
325°	160°
350°	180°
375°	190°
400°	200°
425°	220°
450°	230°
475°	240°
500°	260°

Recipe Testing and Calculating Nutrition Information

Recipe Testing:

- Large eggs and 2% milk were used unless otherwise indicated.
- Fat-free, low-fat, low-sodium or lite products were not used unless indicated.
- No nonstick cookware and bakeware were used unless otherwise indicated. No dark-colored, black or insulated bakeware was used.
- When a pan is specified, a metal pan was used; a baking dish or pie plate means ovenproof glass was used.
- An electric hand mixer was used for mixing only when mixer speeds are specified.

Calculating Nutrition:

- The first ingredient was used wherever a choice is given, such as ⅓ cup sour cream or plain yogurt.
- The first amount was used wherever a range is given, such as 3- to 3½-pound whole chicken.
- The first serving number was used wherever a range is given, such as 4 to 6 servings.
- "If desired" ingredients were not included.
- Only the amount of a marinade or frying oil that is absorbed was included.

America's most trusted cookbook is better than ever!

- 1,100 all-new photos, including hundreds of step-by-step images
- More than 1,500 recipes, with hundreds of inspiring variations and creative "mini" recipes for easy cooking ideas
- Brand-new features
- Gorgeous new design

Get the best edition of the *Betty Crocker Cookbook* today!

www.ingramcontent.com/pod-product-compliance
Lightning Source LLC
Chambersburg PA
CBHW071418290426
44108CB00014B/1872